COMBINED EVENTS

by David Lease
(Scottish National Athletics Coach)

First edition 1971: 'Decathlon' (Tom McNab)
Second edition 1978: 'Decathlon and Pentathlon' (Tom McNab)
This edition 1990

Inside front cover:
Daley Thompson (G.B.) won the gold medal in the Decathlon at the 1980 Olympic Games in Moscow and retained his title four years later in Los Angeles. His performance there, worth 8847 points on the revised scoring tables introduced in 1985, is still the current world record. Daley also won the World Championship at Helsinki in 1983 as well as the European Championship at Athens in 1982 and Stuttgart in 1986, and he won the gold medal at the Commonwealth Games in 1978 (Edmonton), 1982 (Brisbane) and 1986 (Edinburgh).

ISBN 0 85134 094 6 2M/7½M/08.90

Cover photographs of Daley Thompson and Judy Simpson by Allsport.

Designed and printed in England on 115 gsm Fineblade Cartridge by Reedprint Limited, Windsor, Berkshire.

CONTENTS

Author's Note

It is not possible to enjoy competition to the full unless the method of winning and losing, the rules and the boundaries are known and understood.

In writing this booklet it is assumed that the interested party will purchase a copy of I.A.A.F./F.I.A.A. Scoring Tables for Men's and Women's Combined Events Competition and a current I.A.A.F. Handbook which includes the rules for international competition. These can be acquired from:-

The A.A.A./B.A.A.B. Sales Centre,
5 Church Road,
Great Bookham,
Surrey KT23 3PN.

Telephone: 0372 52804

A copy of one's own association handbook is also essential as there are often differences in important detail, e.g. local rules of competition.

A brief chapter of explanation is included in this booklet to identify rules which should not be confused with those of individual athletic events.

Note: The I.A.A.F. Tables include a lengthy history of the development of combined events and an appendix of noteworthy performances, current and historical.

About the Author

David Lease qualified as a Teacher of Physical Education from Cardiff Training College in 1966. He became Scottish National Athletics Coach in 1983 and moved from Culverhay School, Bath, where he was Head of the P.E. Department for twelve years.

As a pole vaulter he represented Great Britain and competed for Wales in two Commonwealth Games. He also represented Wales as a javelin thrower and took part in the 1965 World Trampoline Championships where he placed 9th.

His first major success in coaching came with Robert Hughes in trampolining (British Champion and World Synchronised Champion). Prior to his present post he was B.A.A.B Event Coach for Pole Vault, and he currently coaches a number of British international athletes whose events range from Combined Events to High Jump and Javelin.

Acknowledgements

It would have been a difficult task indeed, to complete this booklet without the expertise and exceptional generosity of the Combined Event experts of Great Britain. Thanks are due to the following people (listed in no particular order):-

Brad McStravick, Bruce Longden, Jim Talbot, Mike Holmes, Doug Frampton, Carl Johnson, Tom McNab and statistician Stan Greenberg for their expertise, acquired by decades of involvement.

Frank Dick, for his patient and expert editing, and Max Jones for his generously donated library.

Athletes Jayne Barnetson, Nicola Emblem, Paul Pentland and Ian Black for their day-to-day assistance.

Mentors, Morton Evans and Sid Aaron.

On behalf of myself and everyone that may benefit from this booklet, thank you!

David Lease

A CONCEPT OF MULTI EVENTS

The Decathlon is rather like having a family of 10 children. You love and want the best for each individual child, but within the framework of the family. Equal devotion leads to harmony, unfairness will inevitably end in disruption and bitterness!

Had a female heptathlete said the same of seven it would be equally true.

One must admire any parent who successfully manages such a large family and recognise that it calls for a person of real talent, not least organisational!

Multi Events requires such a person who will become deeply, even emotionally, involved in each event, striving to achieve personal records but with the vision to view the programme as one event made up of 7 or 10 parts.

Isambard Kingdom Brunel designed each bridge, railway station, even tunnel entrances on the Great Western Railway with loving detail, with an artist's eye, allowing each a little extravagance where possible, never once forgetting that the real aim was to get passengers from Bristol to London in the fastest, safest time. The track was built true and flat. Analogies abound.

The challenge is identified — to score more points at the end of the competition than anyone else.

It is a series of personal challenges — not races. The competition, while against others, is against the tables and oneself. It is therefore not for failed individual eventers but for athletes who thrive in this unique environment.

The object is to improve the whole event, not just the events in it, and it is therefore a task of considerable organisation.

The event will last some 6 to 7 hours for two days. It is an endurance event demanding 7 or 10 peaks of athletic excellence, these peaks completed in only some 7 or 8 minutes work. CONSISTENCY is essential, concentration must be turned on at will. Some events will go well, others are almost bound to be below par. The athlete must bounce back from such an occasion and control his emotions and moods.

Guido Kratschmer (F.R.G.) achieved no personal best performances when making his world record and Daley Thompson had only two in his record breaking effort at the 1984 Olympics.

It would appear that what is initially a physical test is more a test of character and attitude. Certainly if one does not intend to finish one should not start. The multi eventer is positive. There may always be a personal record in the next event of the competition, or to complete under difficult circumstances will help strengthen resolve and gain experience for the future. Such an approach is vital to the successful development of young athletes. Completion may be to honour the competition and fellow competitors, as exemplified by Thompson on his one "off" weekend in 1987. That day the world admired him. He was a complete human being, not just a fantastic competitor.

The Multi Event is the supreme athletic test.

THE COMPETITION

The Multi Event athlete must be confident that the preparation completed to date will produce the performance required. He must put behind him any nagging doubts that there might have been something else that could have been done to gain extra points.

However, just what that performance will entail ought perhaps to be known before one embarks on full scale training for the multi events.

THE PENULTIMATE WEEK

The competition can be lost just as easily in the few days leading up to the physical performance as during the programme itself.

The last very hard sessions of strength training, weight training or plyometrics (hopping and bounding) or strength endurance training should take place about 10 days before the competition. After that, very hard sessions can only detract from the performance.

Some top class decathletes have been known to rest completely in the last week. However, work of the following order is sensible to maintain muscle tone and to give the final touches to skill:

Mon	Hurdles starts over 1, 2 or 3 hurdles 1 × 300m. from blocks flat out
Tues	Long jump run-ups; shot, discus, javelin; high jump
Wed	Sprint starts, pole vault run-up (6 jumps)
Thurs	Rest
Fri	Rest and travel
Sat	Decathlon
Sun	Decathlon

Total preparation for the competition in the last week will amount to:-

Jumps — Full run-ups for Long Jump 3 – 6
,, ,, ,, ,, High Jump 3 – 6
,, ,, ,, ,, Pole Vault 3 – 6

Throws — Shot/Discus — circle discipline; Javelin — run-ups

Running — Starts (hurdles & 100m)
1 × 300m (from 400m start)

Much of the value of the last week's preparation is to ensure a good mental attitude. The athlete must convince himself he is as ready as he could be!

Competitors must be self sufficient for the entire two days of competition. Consequently, everything needed must be replaceable or capable of improvisation, whatever the weather or situation (pole break or snapped shoelace).

Three days beforehand all requirements should be checked against a list. Two days are then available to replace anything missing and a distracting, last minute rush can be avoided.

The bag is best packed the day before the competition and once again each item should be checked against the check list. A slow meticulous approach is best, as displayed by Harold Abrahams (Ben Cross) in the film "Chariots of Fire".

It is always a good idea for the performer to check the track and its condition. The feel of the circles, run-ups, take-off boards, landing areas and their positions should be noted. Check at the latest the night before.

Not only the arena, but toilets, showers, physiotherapists room, rest rooms, shelter available and sources of drink and food must be located.

A CHECKLIST

Towels	— 3 at least
Socks	— 4 pairs — 2 per day
Shorts	— 4 pairs
Vests	— 4
Sweat shirts and sweaters	— cooling is a constant problem!
Tracksuits	— 2 if possible
Waterproof tracksuit	— 1
Training shoes	— 2 pairs preferably
Spikes	— 2 pairs preferably
Specialist event shoes	— high jump shoes, javelin boots, etc. (if available)
Hat	— for sun and rain
Sleeping bag, quilted suit or blanket	— to provide warmth
First Aid	— elastoplast, antiseptic cream
Talcum powder or tape	— for high jump run-up
Spiked marker	— for pole vault and long jump run-up
Measuring tape	— to measure run-ups
Spare pole tips	— for vaulting poles
Tape	— for pole vault grip
Resin	— for pole vault and javelin grips
Old towel	— for wiping throwing implements
Extra screw-in spikes	— variety of sizes (some tracks have a 6mm limit)
Spike spanner	— to change spikes
Pincers	— for the one screw-in spike that will not come out!
Large drink containers	— for sun or rain.

Once again, the reward for such careful preparation will be a positive mental attitude as well as having all practical requirements for the competition.

DAY ONE DECATHLON

(It is recommended heptathlon coaches and athletes also read this section)

Arrival & First Event (100 metres)

The athlete needs to establish himself at the track. All information should be carefully collected and the warm-up begun some one hour beforehand. It will be a slow steady build up of well rehearsed, personal, mental and physical preparation.

10-15 minutes before the event spikes are put on, blocks should be set and some starts practised. Then the best vest is put on with the number attached.

Start of the 1990 Commonwealth Games Decathlon 100 metres (Heat 1).

Fluid Intake

After the 100 metres is a good time for fluid intake; it has been a long time since breakfast. Much physical and nervous energy has been used up and there is still a long time to go. Fruit juice, mineral drink or energy drinks are good, and should be taken as personal thirst and taste require. Above all the athlete must AVOID DEHYDRATION!

Food

Plenty of food as well as drinks must be available. The food should be high energy and hunger suppressing — cakes, buns, yoghurt and honey may suit. Athletes may have to carry their own requirements!

Long Jump

Whatever performance was achieved in the 100 metres is history. What lies before the athlete is in the future and unknown; anything can happen. Some nervous energy has been run off and the athlete can start to apply himself in a more calculating manner.

Warm-up for the long jump can be short. The athlete is already warm from the previous event. One or two relaxed 60 metres runs and full approach run-ups to check the take-off foot in relation to the board, supplemented by a small number of take-off technique drills, should suffice.

It is always worth going over to the long jump runway to mark out the run-up before the "hordes" arrive. It can be done before the 100 metres.

A queue at the Decathlon Long Jump warm-up (Commonwealth Games 1990).

Most top decathletes argue that it is best to go hard at the first attempt and make the necessary adjustments to the run-up thereafter. The warm-up attempts should have given all the information necessary. Each athlete, however, must find his own format for success remembering only three attempts are allowed.

Shot Putt

This event requires its own technical warm-up. Not too many throws should be attempted and the athlete should avoid repeated throwing until a "good one" has been achieved. That throw should be saved for the competition. The first throw should be steady and safe, resulting in a reasonable distance. Once the shot lands inside the sector and a controlled walk out of the back of the circle has been completed, the athlete can try to putt it out of the arena on the final two attempts, safe in the knowledge that points are on the scoresheet.

Immediately after the shot putt and before the high jump is a good time for food and drink.

High Jump

Thirty to forty minutes will be required to prepare thoroughly for this event. The run-up must be marked. A few standing back lay-out jumps, a few run-ups to check the position of the take-off foot followed by a jump at a very safe height, for confidence, will give the athlete the right type of preparation. The athlete may like to jump over a bar at a more realistic height before returning to his sleeping bag. It may be a long competition and it is essential to retain warmth. The aim is to achieve the maximum height with the fewest number of jumps. Energy is a valuable resource!

A safe height should always be cleared before more ambitious attempts are made. Mistakes can be covered if the bar is low. The first competitive attempt could be a long time after the warm-up jump. Athletes should note who jumps four ahead in the jumping order and once he is called, use it as a cue to start preparing. (That athlete may change because some will drop out or simply miss a height. Altertness is essential and the decathlon is a challenge to concentration!!)

Some athletes like to compete against themselves and avoid looking at other jumpers and some like to compete directly against other athletes. Each individual's style should be developed.

It is during the High Jump that the chatting starts. Athletes are around together for a long time. Once again there is no reason why this should not be enjoyed, but concentration must be maintained.

Concentration must be maintained in the High Jump (Jayne Barnetson).

400 metres

A visit to the toilet half an hour before the competition does not display a negative attitude, but commonsense! When warming up the athlete should jog around the track and check the local weather, spotting the strength and direction of the wind. Other cues can be absorbed such as the 200 metres marks, if they are a guide to increasing the tempo.

The event should be run in a controlled, relaxed but fast manner. Fatigue will always be felt after 300 metres but relaxed effort at this stage is vital. Maintenance of good posture and form is crucial in the dying stages of this event.

After the 400 metres a good warm-down is essential. The lactic acid must be got rid of. Lying on one's back cycling legs in the air, jogging a couple of laps, and a good massage, will help enormously. A shower is good, but a hot bath will make the athlete feel good for a short time only and very lethargic the following day. The day is now history. It is a mistake for athletes to stay awake all night attempting to work out the next day's possibilities and they should go to bed when they are ready to sleep.

DAY TWO

Day Two follows the pattern of Day One except for two things:-

a) The bag must be carefully packed again and checked.

b) The 110 metres hurdles will require an extra long warm-up.
   The decathlete will feel he has ossified overnight!

When the athlete arrives at the track, lane draws and competition order must be checked. New numbers may be necessary as the old ones may be ripped or wet.

110m Hurdles

A general warm-up should be followed by a specific hurdle warm-up. In the last 15 minutes some block starts and runs over 1-3 hurdles should be attempted. Five minutes rest before the race to contemplate positive thoughts, resulting in a high level of arousal and a low level of anxiety, will complete an ideal way to start the day.

Immediately after the race plenty of drinks should be taken as on Day One.

Duncan Mathieson (Scotland) warming up for the hurdles on Day Two (9.30 am).

Mens Decathlon 110 metre Hurdles at Commonwealth Games 1990 in Auckland.

Discus

Rather quietly and secretly the discus creeps up on the decathlete and becomes the most critical event. The first throw is quite literally the turning point of the whole two days. It is significant because the athlete moves from a straight line event to a rotational event. The hurdles race is flat out, controlled but entirely aggressive. The discus is slow to start, balletic and graceful. It requires much self control and steadiness. It is for this reason that hurdles and discus are almost always practised in this order in training. The discus requires its own specific warm-up of stretching, standing throws and some rehearsal of the complete action. The first throw should be approached in a steady and controlled manner. The athlete should be almost gentle towards the throw! A reasonable distance is required and the discus must land inside the sector! Once that is achieved the athlete can happily take risks to achieve a personal record.

The athlete should adopt the "four to go" routine of the high jump competition and be ready for each attempt. The particular discus favoured by the athlete should be identified to see where it is, and this may necessitate the athlete going out to the end of the sector to fetch it if it has just been thrown. One's own towel should be used to dry the discus and hands.

The "turning point" of the Decathlon — the Discus.

Pole Vault

The biggest single influence on this event could be the range of ability. 2.30 metre and 5.00 metre vaulters must warm-up together.

The athlete will be getting tired by this stage of the competition, even if he is not aware of it. Measurement of the run-up, checking start and take-off marks and checking the position of the uprights must be done with concentration. The warm-up is similar to the high jump.

It is a good idea to take the first few warm-up attempts from a short approach on a soft pole to ensure confidence.

Only experience will teach the vaulter his trade, but once the warm-up is over and successful (only doing what is normally rehearsed in training), tracksuit and trainers should be put on and warmth, food and drink sought, unless the athlete is one of the unfortunate 2.30 metre vaulters. Watching the bar creep from 2.30m to 3.50m is a mistake. However, frequent checks from a "luxury" viewpoint are necessary to check how high the bar is. A few strides and pole plant drills will be sufficient to regain warmth and the "four to go" routine should be implemented. Athletes will miss heights and the system will be disrupted. Concentration is vital. The first "bar" should be safe and a first time clearance is success! After that the athlete can start vaulting, making minor adjustments as necessary.

Daley Thompson's bar clearance (a metre above his top hand) demonstrates that the early part of the vault must have been technically correct.

As in the long jump, the most accurate run-up is flat out (but relaxed) and the bar and uprights should be moved to suit the athlete. It is fatal to try to adjust the run-up speed to the bar placement. One thought only is acceptable; that of a high plant of the pole! All problems should be sorted out at a height well within the athlete's capabilities. One one occasion Wolfgang Nordwig, Olympic P.V. Champion 1972, entered the competition at 4.60m (cleared first time), took 4.70m (cleared first time), moved to 5.10m for his third height and created a European Indoor best on this fifth vault. He used four different poles throughout the competition and a fifth for his initial warm-up jump. His experience was clearly reflected.

Javelin

At this time the athlete will start to have some idea of the final possible score. However he must concentrate on the task in hand; the javelin. Specific javelin warm-up is important, although the muscle groups are similar to that used in the pole vault. The athlete should take on the persona of the event and feel like a javelin thrower. (The experienced do this with each event.) Plenty of short stabbing throws and some full run-ups to check its accuracy and rehearse the approach will suffice. The athlete should only throw hard if it has been previously proved to be suitable. Some athletes find the first throw is always the best, in which case it should be saved. The order of throwing should be checked and the correct javelin model must be available.

1500 metres

Nothing now stands between the athlete and the worst moment of the competition — the start of the 1500 metres.

The top eight will be in the last heat, the rest in the first heat. Butterflies in the tummy will be experienced. It is the first time direct competition against all the other athletes is experienced. The points required, relative to possible rivals, should be checked and any surmises by opponents should be ignored. They will be lying! A final check that lap times will be called in English and where the caller will be standing is sensible. The athlete should know the lap times needed. There will be pushing and barging.

After the event plenty of social jogging is the order of the day. A good warm-down is advisable.

One day after the competition the athlete may feel good. The next day he will feel awful. At least four days rest is advisable, with plenty of food, before returning to gentle training. Thereafter a gradual return to full training is suggested.

Throughout the competition run-up distances must be known. It is a good idea to write them on the inside of the bag. However learn from the experience of one athlete who wrote her javelin run-up on the side of her javelin boots before the 1986 Commonwealth Games. A few days before the final a well known shoe firm gave the athlete new javelin boots and the old ones were discarded. It must have been disconcerting to realise her run-up measurements were on the old boots in her room while she was in the arena warming-up for the final! All eventualities need to be covered!

THE HEPTATHLON

Virtually all the advice that can be offered to competitors is contained in the section on decathlon. The systematic approach to preparation, arrival and warm-up, even to the two dynamic events on the mornings of Days One and Two, are similar. The fluid intake times, after the first event, are the same and food intake after the High Jump on Day One and Long Jump on Day Two are probably best.

The critical time for Heptathletes often comes with the javelin, unless the athlete is a very competent thrower. The javelins, unlike those of the men, will be distance rated and designed to fly, not to dive into the ground. This means that unless the correct implement is chosen or the point delivered at exactly the correct angle, there is a risk of its landing tail first or "flat" resulting in a foul throw. Athletes and coaches are advised to make certain a suitable javelin is available for competition. This can be done by providing one's own and "checking it in" prior to the competition for weighing and measuring, although this means all athletes can throw it. However this may

Tessa Sanderson, former British Record Holder in the Heptathlon with 6125 pts — 1981 (new scoring tables).

not be possible at major meetings where all javelins are provided by the organisers. A wise coach should contact the B.A.A.B. or "home" association to check which implements the athlete can expect in the competition stadium. The first throw should be made off a controlled approach with a javelin rated below that which will produce the best results, e.g. a 50 metre thrower might throw a 45 metre rated javelin. After the first success caution can be cast to the wind. It is essential to train with the javelin with which one is likely to be confronted in competition.

TABLE 1 Decathlon tables at a glance.

Points	400	500	600	700	800	900	1000	
100 Metres	13.41	12.81	12.26	11.75	11.27	10.82	10.39	seconds
Long Jump	5.09	5.59	6.06	6.51	6.95	7.36	7.76	metres
Shot	8.56	10.24	11.89	13.53	15.16	16.79	18.14	metres
High Jump	1.52	1.65	1.77	1.89	2.00	2.11	2.21	metres
400 Metres	60.40	57.57	54.98	52.58	50.32	48.19	46.17	seconds
110 Metres Hurdles	19.38	18.25	17.23	16.29	15.41	14.59	13.80	seconds
Discus	26.68	31.78	36.80	41.72	46.60	51.40	56.18	metres
Pole Vault	3.18	3.57	3.94	4.30	4.64	4.97	5.29	metres
Javelin	37.06	43.96	50.74	57.46	64.10	70.68	77.20	metres
1500 Metres	5:29.96	5:10.73	4:53.20	4:36.96	4:21.77	4:07.42	3:53.79	minutes

Note: 1) Electrical timing scores have been used for all running events. Please note hand timing scores differ slightly.

2) In this table the performances shown are those nearest to the points score concerned. The actual score in the official tables may be slightly different.

TABLE 2 Heptathlon tables at a glance.

Points	400	500	600	700	800	900	1000	
100 Metres Hurdles	18.90	17.89	16.97	16.12	15.32	14.56	13.85	seconds
High Jump	1.30	1.39	1.49	1.57	1.66	1.74	1.82	metres
Shot	8.01	9.55	11.07	12.58	14.09	15.58	17.07	metres
200 Metres	31.23	29.75	28.40	27.14	25.97	24.86	23.80	seconds
Long Jump	4.39	4.78	5.15	5.50	5.84	6.17	6.48	metres
Javelin	25.92	31.22	36.46	41.68	46.88	52.04	57.18	metres
800 Metres	2:56.38	2:46.60	2:37.70	2:29.47	2:21.77	2:14.52	2:07.63	minutes

Note: 1) Electrical timing scores have been used for all running events. Please note hand timing scores differ slightly.

2) In this table the performances shown are those nearest to the points score concerned. The actual score in the official tables may be slightly different.

UNDERSTANDING THE MULTI EVENT TABLES

Coaches and athletes must have a working understanding of the multi event tables.

The tables are more than a check on competition progress. They are the key to success in the competition and they are the key to planning training. A failure to make the most of the information offered "between the lines" will inevitably lead to disappointment!

TRAINING

The multi events are a compromise, as time and energy are not available in the amounts required to do justice to the full development of the individual events. While the overall programme must be balanced and appropriate to the athlete's status, an understanding of the tables will show those events able to offer the greatest rewards. A 50 point improvement in the decathlon shot putt requires an increase of about 80 centimetres. A similar 50 point improvement in the pole vault is about 17 centimetres and in the long jump approximately 21 centimetres. The coach and athlete may decide, as a result of this study, that a maintenance of shot form and a little extra work on an aspect of long jump or pole vault would be most fruitful. There will be constant updating of the training programme and many adjustments should stem from this form of analysis.

There will also come a time in every multi event athlete's career when an individual discipline is affected by the law of diminishing returns. The amount of work required to make even a small improvement in points becomes unreasonable and would be more productive spent elsewhere. A check of the tables can help identify an athlete's future needs.

COMPETITION

Initially, athletes will be pleased as improvements in performance are rewarded richly. However, after a little experience they will quickly realise that points run away remarkably rapidly if performance is not up to form! The slightest loss of concentration is met with an incredibly cruel drop in points. For example, a young lady who can long jump 6.20 metres but who, because of run-up inconsistency, only manages 5.80 metres loses 121 points!

Understanding of the tables reaches "critical" as the final event becomes imminent. Athletes are also at their most tired! It is vital, for the outcome of the competition, that the athlete knows where he/she is in relation to the opposition.

What is the lead or deficit in points? More importantly, what does that actually represent in seconds, and even more importantly what is that time in terms of metres! A decathlete leading by 50 points can still win the competition despite losing the 1500 metres to his rival, who achieves 4 mins. 21.77 secs (800 pts.) so long as he himself achieves 4 mins. 29.10 secs (751 pts.). However he must know what 7.33 seconds difference represents in metres. If a gap is allowed to develop between them of 35 metres the chances of victory are fast slipping away.

The following table gives a comparison of scores in the 600 to 800 point range.

50 POINTS EQUALS:

Decathlon

100 Mtrs.	Long Jump	Shot	High Jump	400 Mtrs.
.25 sec.	22 cms.	82 cms.	5/6 cms.	1.20 secs.
110 Hurdles	Discus	Pole Vault	Javelin	1500 Mtrs.
.53 sec	2.46 m.	17/18 cms.	3.34 m.	7/8 secs.

Heptathlon

100 Hurdles	High Jump	Shot	200 Mtrs.
.4 sec.	5/4 cms.	75 cms.	.60 secs.
Long Jump	Javelin	800 Mtrs.	
17 cms.	2.6 m.	4 secs.	

PHYSICAL ANALYSIS OF COMBINED EVENTS ATHLETES

An analysis of each event in combined events will help the coach understand why some personal physiques are more advantageous than others.

DECATHLON

There are four obvious and apparently natural divisions within the decathlon, and if points were acquired in a balanced manner the final scores would approximate to the percentages listed:

Sprints	Jumps	Throws	Endurance
100 metres	long jump	shot	1500 metres
400 metres	high jump	discus	
110 metres hurdles	pole vault	javelin	
30%	30%	30%	10%

However points are unlikely to be accumulated in this ideal way and Table 3 and its conclusions demonstrate why.

TABLE 3 Physical requirement analysis — decathlon.

	Aerobic Endurance	Gross Strength	Skill	Relative Strength	Running Speed	Mobility	Explosive Strength	Speed Endurance	Strength Endurance
100m.	Low 2	Med 6	Med 5	High 8	High 10	High 7	High 8	Med 6	Nil 0
Long Jump	Nil 0	Low 4	High 8	High 7	High 9	High 9	High 9	Nil 0	Nil 0
Shot Putt	Nil 0	High 10	High 9	Med 6	Low 3	Med 6	High 10	Nil 0	Nil 0
High Jump	Nil 0	Low 4	High 8	High 8	High 8	High 8	High 8	Nil 0	Nil 0
400m.	Med 5	Low 4	Low 4	High 8	High 9	Med 5	Low 4	Med 5	High 8
110m Hurdles	Nil 0	Med 6	High 10	High 9	High 10	High 10	High 7	Med 6	Nil 0
Discus	Nil 0	High 10	High 10	Med 6	Low 3	High 8	High 8	Nil 0	Nil 0
Pole Vault	Nil 0	Med 5	High 10	High 10	High 8	Med 7	Med 7	Nil 0	Nil 0
Javelin	Nil 0	Med 6	High 10	High 9	Low 4	High 9	High 9	Nil 0	Nil 0
1500m.	High 10	Nil 0	Nil 0	Low 4	Low 3	Nil 0	Nil 0	Nil 0	Med 4

Each element has been scored to a factor of 10.

From the table it can be seen that the decathlon contains many contrasting aspects:

(a) Speed of movement, in high proportions, is required in 9 events (all but the 1500 metres).

(b) Running speed will ultimately limit performance in 5 events, all else being equal (100 metres, 400 metres, 110 metres hurdles, long jump and pole vault).

(c) Skill of an extremely high level is demanded in 3 events (hurdles, pole vault and javelin).

(d) High body mass as required by the discus and shot is detrimental to all other events except the javelin.

(e) Low body mass as required by the 1500 metres is detrimental to all other events.

(f) The predominating requirements are: MOBILITY, SKILL, SPEED and EXPLOSIVE STRENGTH. In short, the multi event athlete must be marvellously AGILE.

Successful performance will therefore depend on a compromise being reached in favour of the explosive events requiring average body mass, with the hope that reasonable points can be gained in the shot and discus and in the 1500 metres, suffering as little as possible!

Physical height is not a disadvantage to any event except arguably sprint starting and is a distinct advantage to most. From a variety of studies 1.88 metres appears to be the average height, although not necessarily the best, for decathletes. Average weight appears to be about 85-90 kilogrammes.

Some successful decathletes:

		height	weight	age (1988)	P.B.
Daley Thompson	GBR	1.85 m	88 kg	30	8847 '84
Jurgen Hingsen	FRG	2.00 m	102 kg	30	8832 '84
Christian Schenk	GDR	2.01 m	93 kg	23	8488 '88
David Steen	CAN	1.88 m	80 kg	29	8415 '88
Torsten Voss	GDR	1.86 m	88 kg	25	8680 '87
Brad McStravick	GBR	1.83 m	85 kg	32	7922w '84

It is important to appreciate that these physiques are the product of many years of participation!

In conclusion the successful performance is likely to breakdown as:

Sprints	Jumps	Throws	Endurance
32%	32.1%	27.1%	8.8%

These figures represent the averages of top twelve performers at the 1988 Olympic Games.

The decathlete, while being many things, is likely to have the appearance of a jumper/javelin thrower.

HEPTATHLON

A similar exercise with the heptathlon displays:-

Sprints	Jumps	Throws	Endurance
100 metre hurdles	high jump	shot	800 metres
200 metres	long jump	javelin	
28.6%	28.6%	28.6%	14.2%

As in the decathlon, points are unlikely to be accumulated in these proportions because some events have contrasting requirements.

TABLE 4 Physical requirement analysis — heptathlon.

	Aerobic Endurance	Gross Strength	Skill	Relative Strength	Running Speed	Mobility	Explosive Strength	Speed Endurance	Strength Endurance
100m. Hurdles	Nil 0	Med 6	High 10	High 9	High 10	High 10	High 7	Med 6	Nil 0
High Jump	Nil 0	Low 4	High 8	High 8	High 8	High 8	High 8	Nil 0	Nil 0
Shot Putt	Nil 0	High 10	High 10	Med 6	Med 6	Med 6	High 10	Nil 0	Nil 0
200m.	Low 4	Med 6	Med 5	High 8	High 10	High 7	High 7	High 10	High 8
Long Jump	Nil 0	Low 4	High 8	High 8	High 9	High 9	High 9	Nil 0	Nil 0
Javelin	Nil 0	Med 6	High 10	High 9	Low 4	High 9	High 9	Nil 0	Nil 0
800m.	High 9	Nil 0	Low 1	Low 4	Med 5	Low 1	Nil 0	Nil 0	High 8

Each element has been scored to a factor of 10.

From the table the following information is apparent:

(a) High speed of movement is essential to all events except the 800 metres.

(b) Running speed is the limiting factor to 3 events, all else being equal (100 metres hurdles, 200 metres and long jump).

(c) Extremely high skill levels are demanded by 2 events (hurdles and javelin).

(d) Anaerobic endurance is required in two disciplines (200 and 800 metres).

(e) High body mass is important to very successful shot putting but detrimental to all the other events (except javelin) which need a balance between strength and bodyweight.

The current heptathlon tables definitely favour the athletes whose bias is towards hurdles and high jump and are least rewarding to javelin throwers and shot putters.

The javelin is something of a peculiarity. Many women find it difficult to throw well, although perhaps it is because they generally practise far less than boys when children. The coach must therefore decide when time and energy might be better utilised elsewhere.

Height is not a necessity to heptathletes but there is no doubt that a tall, well coordinated woman who abounds in speed and elastic strength has a "head start"!

However, some will find the required qualities of skill and power in a compact frame.

Successful heptathletes:

		height	weight	age (1988)	P.B.
Jackie Joyner-Kersee	USA	1.78 m	63 kg	26	7291 '88
Sabine John (Paetz)	GDR	1.74 m	68 kg	31	6946 '84
Anke Behmer	GDR	1.74 m	62 kg	27	6858 '88
Jane Fleming	AUS	1.68 m	57 kg	24	6399 '88
Judy Simpson	GBR	1.82 m	72 kg	28	6623 '86
Kim Hagger	GBR	1.71 m	58 kg	27	6259 '86

In conclusion, the final points distribution for a mature athlete is more likely to be:

Sprints	Jumps	Throws	Endurance
31.7%	30.5%	23.2%	14.7%

These figures represent the averages of the top twelve performers at the 1988 Olympic Games.

It is not by chance that the top class performers probably have the physique of a successful hurdler/jumper.

AGE

Combined event athletes, like good wines, mature with age! Occasionally the greats "show" young . . . Jim Thorpe, Bob Mathias and Daley Thompson . . . but the training is so broad and the skills so diverse that there is always something that can be improved upon. Skills that take a long time to acquire (it is said it takes 7 years to get some idea of a pole vaulter's potential) and physical conditioning over a long period of time give the multi event athletes of greater age a sound platform from which to apply their experience. Assuming they have not accumulated a mass of injuries through incorrect practices when young, of course!

Combined event athletes must be RESILIENT!

TRAINING FOR MULTI EVENTS

The intelligent athlete/coach combination desiring long-term success will want a series of actions and strategies planned well into the future. The further forward from the current moment in time, the broader and more general this plan will become.

Specialisation for Multi Events, as with most athletic activities, is best considered towards the end of the growth spurt, about 14-16 in girls and 16-18 in boys.

At this age the athlete will have entertained reasonable ambitions and will be anxious to participate in the adult world. The physique and potential of the athlete will have developed sufficiently to allow the coach a realistic view.

PRE-SPECIALISATION

"Learning how to learn"

The potential competitors really need some previous involvement of up to two years in track and field as general experience.

It would be hoped that their formative physical education included a broad base, learning many skills in a wide variety of activities and sports, general youthful suppleness and flexibility maintained and a good base of strength and endurance laid from a multitude of general exercises and games. In other words, those activities which encourage healthy growth.

STAGE 1 OF SPECIALISATION

Training to be an athlete: 14-16 girls, 16-18 boys.

The athlete will wish to compete in the next season over a full range of competitions, some of which will be multi events.

The aims of stage 2 should be:-

To prepare for long-term development by:

(a) helping the body to develop further in every possible way.

(b) preparing for Stage 2 in the career of the dec/heptathlete, but including work which will prepare the athlete for next season's competition, especially as this will stimulate interest, help motivate and provide invaluable experience.

The athlete will still be growing and therefore bones will still be soft. Recommended work must take the situation of adolesence into serious account.

Under broad headings the work to be accomplished will be:

Mobility

A full programme of exercises and activities must be developed to allow a full range of movement in all joints of the body. Learning can be impaired by limited mobility. Injuries can result if technical work cannot be completed correctly. Mobility work is vital and should include active, passive and ballistic exercises.

Technique

The fundamentals of running, throwing and take-off should be grooved first.

From there they can be identified in each individual event, which in turn needs to be learned (as opposed to perfected) in a biomechanically correct pattern. In the decathlon special emphasis needs to be placed on the learning of HURDLING, JAVELIN THROWING AND POLE VAULTING. These three events require an abundance of coordination, and if the athlete can progress quickly in at least two and gain good results in the LONG JUMP his career in decathlon looks truly promising. Heptathletes are not quite so pressured as only five events require technique training (7 in the decathlon). Lower hurdle heights and an absence of pole vault relieve the burden considerably, but particular concentration on HURDLES, HIGH JUMP and JAVELIN in the technical sessions at this stage will be well rewarded.

The multi event athlete must spend more time rehearsing complete techniques correctly and pay less attention to isolated drills than the specialist event athlete. Time and energy are in limited supply; however that must not be used as an excuse for indifferent techniques.

Speed

It is absolutely vital that the foundations of SPEED be laid early, particularly running speed. Eastern block research suggests 10-14% of the total workload should be towards the improvement of speed. As techniques improve speed can be applied in a controlled manner. Alternating between correct rehearsal of movement and performing at speed will be a constant occurrence as the correct technical pattern cannot be sustained under pressure.

Strength

is required to:

(a) complete each event technique correctly

(b) give a sound base for further development.

The muscles which support and give the spine its flexibility, abdominals, rotational muscles of the trunk, the muscles attached to the spine and pelvic girdle and the spine and shoulder girdle must all be strengthened first to provide a strong platform for powerful limb movements, prevent injury and protect vital body organs. Body weight exercises within a dynamic circuit constitutes the best form of training. Some weight training, especially for rarely used muscle groups, is useful. These weights should be light, 40-70% of a ten repetition possible maximum. All strength work should be done with many repetitions. (If an athlete can complete a minimum of ten repetitions under control it suggests the muscles are being stressed, rather than ligaments and bone structure distressed.)

Endurance

Endurance training is important, not for immediate improvement for the 1500, although there will be a spin off, but to prepare the body to cope with the vast amount of work to be overcome in the future.

The work should be mainly aerobic with large volumes of low intensity anaerobic work, e.g. repetition 150's-300's.

STAGE 2 OF SPECIALISATION

Training to be a decathlete/heptathlete: 16-19 women, 18-21 men

The general education should be complete and the athlete's potential can now be recognised.

The aim of Stage 2 is to lay the foundation for the achievement of personal potential and to give the athlete the physical equipment necessary to compete and survive in the tough world associated with high performance.

A large volume of strength training must be built into the training programme to improve the quality (speed) of running and jumping and, of course, throwing. Anaerobic running is given greater emphasis, and with this comes a further basis for running improvement.

A mastery of all techniques (as opposed to learning) is sought.

Periodising an athlete's year will start in earnest and with effect in Stage 2.

Mobility

A rolling programme should be underway, but special emphasis needs to be placed on the requirements of each individual event.

Technique

As a result of work done in Stage 1, increased strength and endurance will permit the athlete to perform through wider ranges of movement and with more power. Immature techniques need to be expanded to adult capabilities. Consequently, rhythms will change and these must be mastered and strengthened.

Complete exercises and related specialised drills must be practised, eventually under competition conditions.

All techniques must remain simple and basic.

Speed

As the overall volume of work is increased, care must be taken to avoid an easing in quality which will result in a dropping off of speed. It cannot be stressed enough that balance must be maintained between speed, strength, endurance and technique training. An over-emphasis on strength or endurance could ultimately spell disaster. SPEED IS THE VITAL FACTOR GOVERNING SUCCESSFUL MULTI EVENTS.

To maintain progress the intensity of the speedwork should be increased but the volume of work decreased.

Speed activities:

- speed in jumping
- speed in throwing
- sprint accelerations
- changes in tempo
- sprint from low starts & walking
- reaction training
- relaxation training.

It is suggested that 10-20% of the total work done should be on speed.

In the "preparation for competition" phase, speedwork in small regular doses every week will have a beneficial effect on speed and also help unite the training as a whole.

Strength

Strength work will change from general work to the development of specific strength.

The volume and the intensity should be increased using weight training and other dynamic methods but **it is vital to remember that explosive strength is the ultimate aim.** A system of 6-8 repetitions of 3-5 sets is best, supported by dynamic, bodyweight circuits. There should be a gradual increase in plyometric work (elastic strength, i.e. hopping and bounding) moving towards measured performances.

Endurance

Emphasis moves to the anaerobic system. However aerobic endurance training will always be essential to the multi eventer. Low intensity, steady running therefore remains an important part of the programme.

STAGE 3 OF SPECIALISATION

19+ Women and 21+ Men

The aim is to realise potential and produce performances of the highest quality.

To this end:

Mobility — is directly related to each event.

Techniques — should become automatic and merely extensions of reflexes. However, the athlete should attempt to learn advanced subtleties. Practice will be more related to competition rehearsal and will include psychological preparation.

Speed & Strength — should move closer together and will include advanced plyometrics and complex training (weight training alternating with plyometrics and event training), especially in the pre-competition phase. Programmes will be very individualised. Speed is still the central link and over emphasis on strength or endurance can disrupt consistency or even lead to injury.

PLANNING TRAINING SCHEDULES FOR MULTI EVENTS

The organisation and the principles by which athletic training is organised is comprehensively covered in "Training Theory" by Frank Dick (B.A.A.B. Publications). However the decathlon and heptathlon are complicated events and it is important to understand how the subject relates to these events.

PRINCIPLES OF TRAINING

1) Over Compensation

It is vital to appreciate that improved athletic performance is the result of TRAINING AND RECOVERY. Training on its own will simply exhaust the body. The body's natural reaction to physical stress is to rebuild tired or damaged parts stronger than before. This rebuilding is done during recovery. The length of recovery required depends on the severity of the stress placed on the body and the type of body cell stressed, e.g. muscle cells (fibres) recover much more quickly than nerve cells.

The amount of work an athlete can productively accept will be quite individual to that athlete and will depend on numerous factors such as age, sex, experience, stage of physical development, and the regularity with which an activity is practised. There are many other factors to be taken into account and consequently coaching is currently an art based on science.

RECOVERY MUST BE BUILT INTO THE TRAINING SCHEDULE AS A MAJOR COMPONENT.

2) Specific Training produces Specific Results

The body only improves in the manner and direction in which it has been trained.

This has very serious implications for multi eventers where the number of activities to be trained are many and most of them are explosive, consuming vast amounts of energy. Coaches should find as many common core activities as possible.

3) Intensity versus Volume

Explosive work such as sprinting, hopping and bounding (plyometrics) and actual event practice (except endurance) require high outputs of energy in short periods of time. They are therefore intense. By their very nature they are highly technical activities and the athlete needs to be fresh to complete them accurately. Adequate rest between trials is vital. They are usually completed within the alactic-anaerobic energy system. There is a limit to how much of this high grade work the body can accept and therefore the volume of work will be relatively low.

The better the body is conditioned the higher that volume will be, and because combined event athletes need to cover such a broad spectrum of activities at the highest intensity possible they need to be extremely well-conditioned. Large volumes of strength training and endurance running (both aerobic and anaerobic) must be completed.

It is obvious that the two types of activity are incompatible; therefore where action is intense the volume should be low and when the volume is high the intensity must be low.

Should the coach underestimate the importance of this general rule, the athlete will flirt with injuries, accidents and illness.

CONSTRUCTING A TRAINING SESSION

Training programmes will be composed of (for simplicity) 5 'S's':

Suppleness
Skill
Speed
Strength
Stamina

It is suggested that training sessions are completed in this written order until the coach is experienced and understands why, and when, this order may be overruled.

The reasons for this order are logical and closely allied with the rule of intensity/volume:

(a) A session must start with a warm-up, part of which should be suppling (mobility) work. Some skills cannot be completed correctly if mobility is restricted.

(b) Skill (technique) training requires the performer to be fresh and able to concentrate to be effective. Tired performers make mistakes!

(c) Speed, either on the track or within other technical events, is an extension of technique and by definition, very intense. As a result of tiredness, the activity will cease to be speed but become strength endurance.

(d) Strength work will cause fatigue and will affect the quality of any of the previously mentioned activities if it precedes them in the daily programme. Endurance training produces pronounced fatigue and any attempted strength training that follows will inevitably be endurance rather than power based!

(e) Endurance, for the multi event athlete, is therefore left to conclude the day's training.

The coach must ensure his definition of an activity is accurate. He must also appreciate that practices can contain more than one quality, e.g. a pole vault session will be a skill or technique session but it will also undoubtedly be a strength session.

The particular day's training must also take into account the type of training undertaken on previous days.

PLANNING A NUMBER OF DAYS' TRAINING (A MICROCYCLE)

A similar pattern, following the order of the 5 'S's, can be adopted with the same logical reasoning when putting together a number of training days.

Day 1 Rest
Day 2 Suppleness, Skill (technique learning), Speed
Day 3 Strength
Day 4 Stamina
Repeat

The high intensity activities follow a day of rest to ensure correct participation and to avoid injury.

Injury will always threaten when speed training follows the day after heavy strength training of similar muscle groups!

This programme is very simplistic and should be adapted to the actual situation.

The average 16-17-year-old may undertake the following, assuming he/she is suitably prepared and facilities and personnel are available. All sessions must be preceded by an adequate warm-up and completed with a warm-down:

Day 2 Mobility, Technique 1, Speed, Strength (explosive)

Day 4 Mobility, Technique 2, Strength, Endurance

Day 6 Mobility, Technique 3 (to include speed), Strength

Day 7 Mobility, Endurance

Days 1, 3, 5, 8 Rest

The good club athlete of senior status can take on a more comprehensive week's work. If the rule of specificity is carefully observed and planning is astute, the following is possible:

Day 1 Rest

Day 2 Technique 1, Speed 1, Strength 1 (explosive)

Day 3 Technique 2, Strength 2 (endurance)

Day 4 Endurance 1

Day 5 Active Recovery

Day 6 Technique 3, Speed 2, Strength 1 (repeated)

Day 7 Strength 2 (repeated), Endurance 2

PLANNING A NUMBER OF WEEKS' TRAINING (A MESOCYCLE)

Many well prepared athletes find it very rewarding to be involved in a cycle of hard training for three weeks and light training for the fourth week. Eastern Bloc sprint coaches have offered even more specific information to their athletes regarding the intensity of their work:

Week 1 intensity = 95% of maximum effort.

Week 2 ,, = 100% ,, ,, ,,

Week 3 ,, = 95% ,, ,, ,,

Week 4 ,, = 25% ,, ,, ,,

Organisation of a four-week workload in this manner allows:

(a) Recovery to be built into the programme.

(b) The body to operate in conjunction with its natural biological rhythms.

(c) Monthly targets.

(d) A manageable period of time to plan.

Coaches may wish to modify this pattern to accommodate younger or less well prepared athletes by adopting a two-week cycle: one hard week, one easy week, especially at times of transition.

Two or three similar mesocycles, progressively planned, can be worked consecutively to form a macrocycle, especially during winter preparation.

The coach should appreciate that the athlete may, or may not, perform well on the first day of the new month (the day after a light week). The very best performance may be delivered after a few days of more vigorous training. This has serious implications for competition preparation.

THE YEAR PLAN

Dividing the training year into phases is known as periodisation. It is possible to have a single periodised year or a double periodised year. In most instances multi events athletes would be advised to adopt a single periodised year because of the volume of work that must be undertaken. However that does not exclude the athlete from mid-winter competition as training for multi events is something of a special case.

Table 5

Single Periodised Year:

months	Nov	Dec	Jan	Feb	Mar	Apr	May	Jun	Jul	Aug	Sep	Oct
phases	1				2		3		4	5		6
periods	preparation						competition					transition

Double Periodised Year:

months	Nov	Dec	Jan	Feb	Mar	Apr	May	Jun	Jul	Aug	Sep	Oct
phases	1_1		2_1	3_1	1_2		2_2	3_2	4	5		6
periods	preparation			comp.	preparation			competition				transition

The phasing-periodising of the year against the months indicated is a suggestion for illustration. Commencement of the "year" will vary according to individual circumstances and requirements.

Success in the decathlon or heptathlon depends heavily on consistency of performance and by maintaining a balance between the individual events.

Consequently it is to the athlete's advantage to ensure that technical work progresses steadily alongside that of speed and strength throughout the year.

It is a more efficient use of time and energy to keep the critical timing of crucial techniques well "serviced" during conditioning periods because there are so many techniques involved.

Variations in speed affect such timings, and so the astute coach will include some high quality speed work in the programme from week five of the training year onwards.

Similarly, a sudden increase in speed just prior to competition is not necessarily advantageous. It will gain good points in the 100 metres but could ruin rhythm and judgement on approach runs, especially when one remembers that only three attempts are allowed in multi event long jump and throws.

The individual event techniques should be settled to competition standard well before the pre-competition phase begins. This latter phase should be devoted to ensuring events can be successfully performed in competition order. (Some coaches insist event practice always takes place in competition order; however it should be appreciated that if this system is strictly adhered to many events will never enjoy prime training time, i.e. when the athlete is most alert and receptive.)

It is for these reasons that a multi event athlete can take on some winter competition, although perhaps it should be viewed as a high quality training session and a progress check rather than a test of competitive form. Certainly winter competition acts as an incentive and as a target in the long winter months.

In conclusion, the year's work for a multi event athlete is unlikely to vary from phase to phase to the extent that single event preparation might. One month's training will undoubtedly be extremely varied, but monthly variations are likely to be noticeable through changes in loadings rather than changes of basic principles.

Table 6 Organisation of the major types of training. Status — Senior Club Athlete.

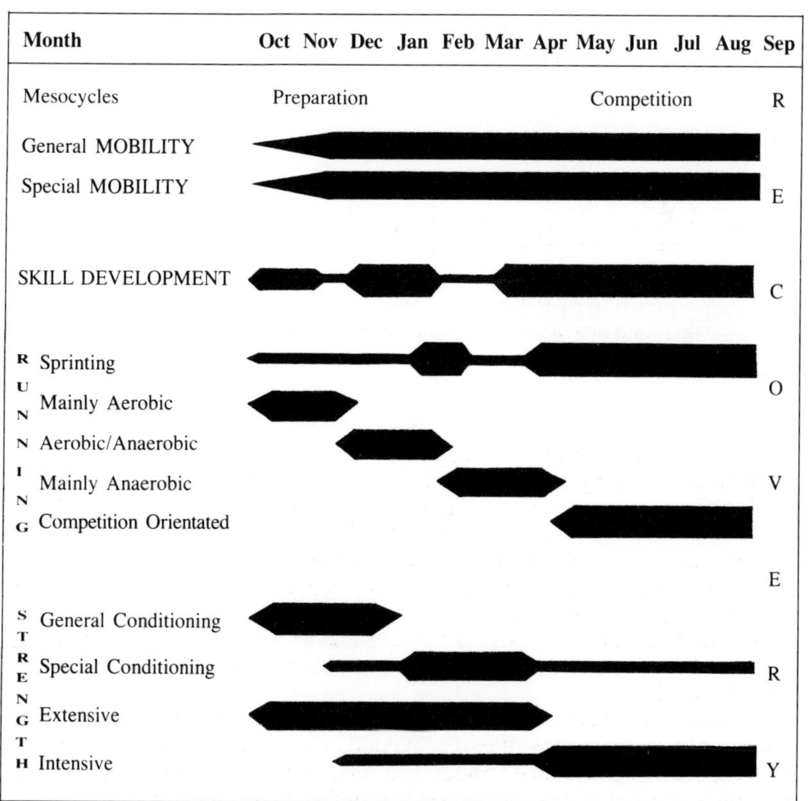

THE CONTENT OF TRAINING PROGRAMMES

1) TECHNICAL TRAINING

The coach should be able to observe the following if the athlete competes in a multi event competition after one year of specialisation:

N.B. Not in competition order.

100 metres	block start — signs of good running technique — run through the tape.
200/400 metres	block start — controlled run.
800/1500 metres	signs of pace control.
100/110 hurdles	block start — correct hurdle action — 3 stride pattern.
Long jump	standing start to run-up — measured 14 stride approach — correct take-off action.
Pole vault	standing start to run-up — measured 10/14 stride approach — correct plant/take-off action — swing — simple turn and pole pushed away.
High jump	standing start to run-up — measured 6/8 stride approach, 3 on final curve — correct take-off action — flop.
Shot	2 throws from power position — final throw with shift.
Javelin	standing start to run-up — 1 throw from 5 strides — high arm action — final throw from full 4-2-3 run-up.
Discus	2 throws from power position — final throw from one turn.

While the coach should be able to observe the correct technical movements the ATHLETE MUST BE ABLE TO COMPETE IN A RELAXED MANNER THAT ENHANCES HIS/HER NATURAL FLAIR. As a result his/her "style" might not mirror exactly the classic text book action.

(Bruce Jenner cleared 4.87 metres (16′) in the pole vault from the wrong take-off foot while winning the decathlon at the Montreal Olympics! As a young man he had taught himself to pole vault and by the time he discovered the correct technique he, wisely, decided his own action was too ingrained to change.)

TECHNICAL PROGRESS

A layman's guide to learning techniques is that if rhythm and skills are to be maintained, practice once a week is adequate. However, if improvement is sought, twice weekly practice is the minimum. A short burst of three sessions per week, for a few weeks, is ideal when seeking rapid improvement. A few days between sessions is invaluable as the athlete seems to remember the good and forgets the bad.

Technical progress will not be made smoothly, but in plateaus and jumps with occasional troughs. The athlete should also be aware of this!

TECHNICAL SESSIONS

During development the coach must look for sessions that will benefit as many events as possible.

1) Running

Posture runs over 40-60 metres at 80% of maximum speed concentrating on:

(a) running tall, relaxation

(b) correct arm carriage

(c) leg action — pushing

(d) leg action — striking

Specialist sprinter Linford Christie demonstrates "Model Sprint Technique".

All runs to be made from a standing start (as in all run-ups).

Decathletes could do every fourth session carrying a vaulting pole.

Initially 20 minute sessions should take place twice per week, but once understood this practice should become part of the warm-up (during jogging and striding).

Block Start — Eugene Gilkes, Bronze Medalist Decathlon 1990 Commonwealth Games.

2) Block Starts

Once learned this activity can be revised intermittently, especially in the pre competition phase and during the competitive season. It must be regularly practised in conjunction with hurdles.

3) Jumping, Take-offs

All take-offs require:

Posture	— tall
Take-off foot action	— active
Take-off leg action	— strike
Free leg action	— drive
Hip position	— rolled under
Trunk position	— upright and stable
Head position	— natural
Approach rhythm	
Balance	

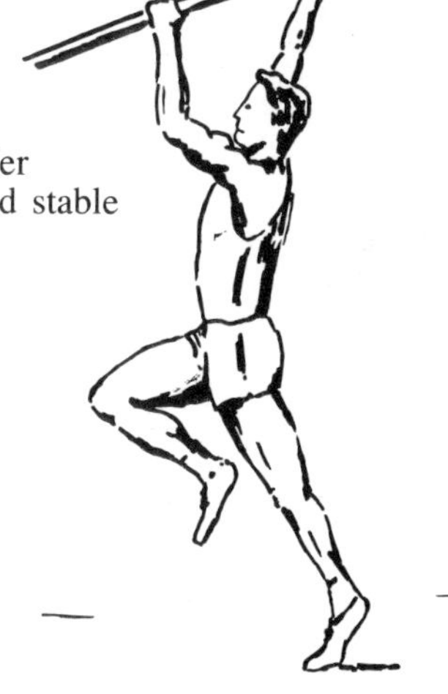

Jumps Take-offs.

These movements are similar for all the jumps (despite different approaches).

The differences are:

high jump — double arm action
long jump — single arm action
pole vault — pole push arm action

10/15 minute sessions on general take-offs can be followed by a specific jump session.

4) Throwing from the Power Position

All throwing requires:

- Correct feet placement — hip width apart (when viewed from front or back).
- Transfer of weight from back foot through and over front foot.
- A complete body action ensured by continued outward rotation of the rear heel.
- A braced opposing side with high shoulder ensured by straightening of the front leg against the throw.
- The necessary arm action.
- The throw to be completed by delivering the implement from "low" to "high".

Entry to the power position is different for each throw:

Javelin — from a run
Discus — from a rotational turn
Shot — from a reverse shift

The power position in the three throws.

Throwing, Hurling and Putting sessions that reinforce the basic throwing action can be included before event practice to help avoid duplication.

THE ABOVE PRACTICES ARE COMMON CORE PRACTICES AND SHOULD SUPPLEMENT, NOT SUBSTITUTE FOR, PRACTICE AT EACH INDIVIDUAL EVENT.

INDIVIDUAL EVENT SESSIONS

Events within the heptathlon and decathlon require varying amounts of energy output and varying amounts of time to maximise their performance. Some events deserve more attention than others because the rewards, in terms of points, are greater.

Some events are worthy of more time because they contain many common factors.

Sprinting — is the key to multi events. It does not require a great deal of time and does not have a negative effect on any event. It is, however, the main source of injury. Two speed sessions a week would seem reasonable for development.

Long Jump — is a highly rewarded event in both heptathlon and decathlon. It is closely allied to sprinting and does not require extreme strength or large body mass. Shorter approach runs in all the jumps compared to those of jumps specialists are suggested. This is to ensure consistency. Standing starts are recommended for the same reason. Short but regular sessions of specific long jumping are recommended.

Hurdles — is the key event for women and almost as important for men. It has a good carry over value to other events. Special attention needs to be paid to hurdling. Daily hurdle drills and mobility work can be slotted into warm-up routines, even when preparing for other activities. Hurdle sessions with and without block starts need to be frequent.

Specialist Hurdler Colin Jackson attacks the hurdle.

Sally Gunnell, 13th at the European Junior Heptathlon Championships 1984 (5493 pts new scoring tables), maintains high hips off the hurdle.

Javelin — is another event that requires specific all year round practice because the high speed of movement involved requires such precise coordination. Regular sessions of 20/40 throws of varying effort are required.

Pole vault — for the men, requires at least once a week training all through the year, with frequent (but not exclusive) practice on a pole near competition "flex". The good pole vaulter is well rewarded with points and the event, like hurdles, has a good carry over to other events as it contains so many common factors. Five metres is quite achievable for fast mobile athletes. 15/20 vaults on progressively stronger poles 1/2 times per week are essential.

High Jump — if learned effectively when young, seems to require less attention. Terrific stress is placed on the knee and ankle at take-off and practice should be intermittent for the mature athlete.

Correct foot placement is essential to avoid stress in the ankle, knee and hip joints.

Discus — is a tricky event and 20/30 throws throughout the year twice a week would afford great assistance to the athlete's balance.

Shot — requires large body mass to progress beyond certain levels. The event is not well rewarded in terms of points. However in the learning stages the throwing action has good carry over value to the other throws. Initial training should be frequent, but once learned training can be intermittent.

Daley Thompson entered decathlon training having already achieved 10.8 for the 100 metres, 6.80 metres for the long jump and 1.90 metres for the high jump. He had never attempted five of the other seven events.

Bruce Longden, who coached Daley to his first Olympic gold medal, resolved the problems of balancing the technical side of training in the following way:

Development Cycles		Event Emphasis	
Common Factors		*Special Emphasis*	*Less Emphasis*
1974/75	running (AN, AER) strength technique mobility	technique work on: discus shot pole vault	 high jump long jump javelin
1975/76	as above	pole vault high jump discus	shot javelin
1976/77	as above plus more strength work	pole vault long jump hurdles high jump	discus javelin
			shot
1977/78	,,	pole vault hurdles javelin high jump	long jump discus
			shot
1978/79	,,	hurdles discus javelin shot	pole vault high jump long jump
Future		pressure events	

AND EXAMPLE OF THE WINTER EMPHASIS OF A CYCLE

Macrocycle		Microcycles
	Common factors	*Events*
NOV.	mobility, strength, endurance	PV, Shot, Hurdles
DEC.	and speed	PV, Shot, LJ
JAN.	,,	PV, LJ, Discus, HJ
FEB.	,,	PV, DT, HJ, Hurd
MAR.	,,	PV, DT, Hurd, LJ

NOTE: Basic technique training is explained in detail in "BUT FIRST" by F.W. Dick (B.A.A.B. Publications) and detailed further in the B.A.A.B. series of 'event' books. This chapter should be seen as a guide to this further information.

SPEED TRAINING

Speed runs like a motorway through the heart of the multi events. We have already stressed it is an all-the-year-round activity, except during rest and preliminary preparation phases. Speed is an extension of techniques but dependent on strength and flexibility. Running speed can be improved by either increasing stride rate or increasing stride length. Great sprinters apply similar power as lesser mortals but in less contact time with the track. Training for speed involves conditioning the nervous system as much as the muscular system.

Sprint sessions should include:

— Acceleration runs 60-100 metres
— Starts to 30 metres
— Up & down the clock, e.g. — 100m, 110m, 120m, 130m, 140m, 150m, 140m, 130m etc.
— 6 × 100 metres
— Run-ups with or without taking off
— Stride frequency runs
— Indoor competition
— Early season competition
— Sprint drills

Overspeed work includes:

— Wind-assisted sprinting
— Runs catapulted by elastic

All runs in sessions requiring speed must, by definition, be separated by ample amounts of rest, i.e. at least 3 to 5 minutes.

ANAEROBIC ENDURANCE RUNNING

Decathletes ought to complete approximately half the workload of the 400 metre specialist with regards to anaerobic endurance. There is no reason for women to have a different attitude to the men as this activity benefits both the 200 and 800 metres events directly and all but the two throws indirectly.

Through the winter months two anaerobic running sessions complemented by one sprint session is ideal. (A second sprint session is likely to be undertaken as part of a jump session.)

November through December from:-

6 × 150 metres, jog recovery
6 × 200 metres, jog recovery
4 × 300 metres, 4/5 minutes recovery between runs

January / February:-

6 × 200 metres
3 × 300 metres
6 × 150 metres

March / April

Speed should be increased, recovery should be increased.

4 × 200 metres
4 × 150 metres
2/3 × 300 metres
6 × 100 metres

These sessions should not be so stressful that a hurdle session (men) or a long jump session (women) could not be completed the following day.

ENDURANCE

General endurance running should be undertaken by the multi event athlete throughout the year, not just to improve the specific events 800/1500 metres but to improve general capacity for work, to maintain conditioning, and as active recovery.

Winter — 20/40 minutes steady (low intensity) running or
Diagonals (jog the goal line, run from corner to corner) of a football pitch, 20/40 minutes or
Similar aerobic sessions.

These sessions can be very monotonous to the multi eventer who probably came into the event because he/she enjoyed variety or wished to express talent for coordinational activities. The coach must use all his initiative to find interesting venues and ways of maintaining enthusiasm.

Soviet athletes answered the problem by completing two kilometres of steady running before and after each day's training, amounting to about 100 kilometres per month!

As the season approaches, sessions to prepare the athlete for the specific task of 800/1500 metres can start.

Men — once per week from:-
1200 metres time trial
1000 " " "
3 × 800 metres with short recovery
800 metres jog/800 metres fast 2.30 mins./800 metres jog
3 × 500 metres at race speed

Women — 3 × 300 metres at 800 metres speed
4 × 400 " " " " "
600 metres / 200 metres at 800 metres speed

STRENGTH TRAINING

Strength requirements for a multi event athlete are many.

1) Torso Strength

A strong and stable trunk is required to act as a platform from which dynamic limbs can generate power.

Examples:

Crunches
Back Raises
Side Bends
Single Leg Raises, Backwards

2) Bodyweight Circuits

Dynamic circuit exercises using only the body weight make up the initial strength exercises for the beginner and need to be continued throughout the athlete's career. Exercises need to be selected with care so that they ensure balanced development of the body. The abdominals usually require special attention and exercises for them, the back, the rotational muscles of the trunk, the shoulder girdle, the pelvic girdle and the legs should all be identifiable in the circuit.

From:

Chinnies
Treadmills
Sit-ups
Burpees
Star jumps
Bench astride jumps
Alternate step jumps, bench
Press-ups
Pull-ups
etc.

3) Weight Training

Weight training can be used for a variety of purposes.

It also has the advantage of being measurable and therefore can be systematically progressive.

Athletes, particularly young ladies, should not fear that it will make them "big and muscley" as long as the weights are moved dynamically.

(To become bigger, the participant is required to lift slowly and must have a talent for becoming big. Some athletes may need to include such sessions in their preparation phase at some stage of their career, but multi event athletes are not body builders and bulk is detrimental to all events except the throws.)

(a) Weight training to increase strength and power in specific muscles and muscle groups which are unmanageable with whole body exercises:-

Straight or bent arm pullovers	—	pole vault & javelin
Arm curls	—	,, ,, ,,
Upright rowing	—	,, ,, ,,
Inclined press	—	shot & pole vault
Bent arm flys	—	discus
Wrist curls	—	pole vault & all throws
Leg extension	—	all events
Thigh curl	—	all events
Calf raises	—	all events

(b) Weight training to increase leg power:-

Half squats
Quarter squats
Front squats
Cleans
Snatch
Leg press

The nature of these exercises allows much greater resistance to be used.

SAFETY

Weight training has its rules to ensure safe participation, as do all activities, and both the coach and athlete must know and implement them.

The beginner is advised to work on multigym type equipment. He/she is also advised not to load the spine or press overhead until the bone structure is mature.

A minimum of ten repetitions is advised for the physically immature.

Two sessions a week of 6/10 exercises are recommended during the winter, and at least one session in the summer to maintain strength gains.

The experienced, mature athlete can progress to:-

During the preparation phase,

(a) 8, 6 or 4 repetitions with increased weight × 4/6 sets

(b) Pyramid lifts, 8 repetitions, followed by 6 repetitions, 4 and finally two repetitions, all with progressively higher loads.

During the pre-competition phase and competition phase,

(a) "timed" sets of 6 seconds, with the lifts to be completed rapidly, using 75% of the weight used in sets of 6 without a time limit.

(b) Once a fortnight a winter session, using 95% of winter loadings, can be undertaken to maintain strength.

The coach needs to employ variety when constructing schedules to maintain enthusiasm and to stimulate the necessary biological responses.

4) Explosive Strength

Hopping and bounding

Hopping left leg
Hopping right leg
High skips
Long skips
Bounds
Straight leg runs
High knees
Bunny jumps (90 degree bend of the knee)

These activities can form a routine using 6/8 contacts per exercise, a walkback recovery between exercises, and 5 minutes recovery between sets. The number of sets used will depend on the athlete's maturity. Two sets is ample for beginners.

Alternatively

Combinations of hops and bounds

4 hops and a jump
hop, step, hop, step, etc.
See — Jumps Decathlon, tables provided in "BUT FIRST".
See — Jumps Quadrathlon

Hurdle Bounds

Two-footed jumps over 6 hurdles — 3/4/5 sets
Hurdle skips — Hop over the hurdle and step between.

Stadium Step Bounding

Running, bounding, hopping and jumping up suitably spaced stadium steps provide excellent explosive leg strengthening exercises. However, great care should be taken coming down, because of the eccentric nature of the work.

Other explosive leg work

Hill runs, 30/60 metres sprint (3/10 degree incline) × 5/10
Tyre towing, 30/60 metres × 5/10
Towing against elastic and partner × 5/10.

Medicine Ball Throwing

Overhead throw, from two feet (soccer throw-in)
Overhead throw, one foot forward
Overhead throw, rear knee on floor
Putting as above
Hurling, one arm, right and left, two feet together
" " " " " " one foot forward
" " " " " " sitting
Overhead backward throwing
etc.

Ten repetitions per throw with 3 minutes recovery between sets. The number of sets depends on the maturity of the athlete.

A routine of this nature, if done with a very light ball, can be used as a technique session.

Complex Training

The mature athlete can combine hopping and bounding and weight training lifts, or medicine ball throwing and weight training lifts alternatively as one session:-

One set of hurdle bounds followed by one set of squats × 6.

Note! This type of training is very demanding and very rewarding, but not for the ill prepared or the immature.

MOBILITY

Sessions should be part of every day warm-up and warm-down and must include specific mobility for each event. Exercises for the hurdles and javelin are vital and need to be part of the daily routine. The athlete would be wise to devote some sessions weekly to the improvement or maintenance of a high standard of mobility, especially during days allocated to active recovery. The B.A.A.B. devotes an entire booklet to Mobility Training, written by Norman Brook.

THE ROLE OF THE MULTI EVENT COACH

The aim of any coach is to help the athlete to prepare for, arrive at, compete in and finally learn from the overall experience. However the multi event coach will be faced with problems not normally experienced by other athletic coaches. It is unlikely that he will have either the time or the expertise in each individual event to cover the complete operation himself. He will be a MANAGER.

The coach must have the responsibility, with the athlete, of planning and preparing the overall training and competition programme in detail. Training theory must be understood. He must be able to coach a number of events himself and develop the ability to (a) identify and (b) involve other coaches who can complement his talents. He must be able to delegate!

It is not easy to enlist the correct assistance. The assistant coach and the athlete have to be compatible. The assistant coach needs to appreciate and sympathise with the philosophy of multi event training and that the athlete has limited time and energy!

The session, which is likely to be for technique, can only be short — 20/30 minutes. Its contents must be restricted to basics, which need to be taught extremely well. Anything else is extra! Consistency is all important. It is better to work, for example, with slightly shorter run-ups as time wasted on possible aborted approach runs is too expensive. It is good coaching practice to expect a beneficial result from each time an exercise is started!

The multi event coach should attempt to attend as many of the sessions conducted by an assistant coach as possible to:

(a) ensure complete communication is exchanged

(b) advance his own knowledge

(c) check if practices can be duplicated with other events.

The multi event coach must help the athlete to organise his/her competition programme. Liaison with club officials is essential if the athlete is not to be over worked! Both athlete and club may have to compromise as the club would like the athlete to cover as many events as possible (especially less popular ones) and the athlete would like to practise specific events. Three events and a relay is the advised maximum to do justice to both athlete and club but even so, event times must be adequately spread out to allow for correct event warm-ups to take place. Injury will be the almost certain outcome if, for example, the athlete is expected to throw the javelin without a proper warm-up. It is not acceptable for the athlete to run between events that share the same slot on the timetable.

The coach would be wise to ensure that the athlete is able to compete in the competitions he/she has prepared for by:-

(a) ensuring the athlete has completed and posted entry forms,

(b) ensuring the athlete can reach the venue. Vaulting poles may cause problems!

The multi event coach may find coaching a group very effective. A group spirit can be developed which acts as a carrot to help athletes through tough times. Athletes will learn from one another and will be more inclined to follow the group and partake in the less attractive moments training requires.

Correctly educated, the group can give one another technical advice when the coach is unavailable. A good group will even revitalise the coach if his enthusiasm flags!

The multi event coach needs to be flexible in approach and enjoy variety. He needs to be generous, especially with time, and have an accurate opinion of his own ability. Above all he must be able to gather a team of people about him, lead them, direct them and motivate them.

The multi event coach will know the rules, will know the tables and will eventually know the basis of all the events.

THE HISTORY OF MULTI EVENTS

MEN

The likelihood is that competitions for the best all-rounder have created excitement for as long as humans have enjoyed competition. They are natural. Most sports have them: Nordic sports, water sports, track and field; even cricket, a team game, has a competition to find the best "all-rounder".

History records a pentathlon in the Classical Greek Olympic Games which comprised: long jump, discus throw, javelin throw, 192 metre sprint and wrestling — 2600 years ago.

Modern Olympic track and field sprang from the Much Wenlock Olympics which included, in 1857, a pentathlon of: high jump, long jump, 36lb shot putt, 880 yard run and 55ft rope climb.

The first Olympic Multi Event competition was the unofficial decathlon at the St. Louis Olympic Games. This was made up of: 100 yards, shot putt, high jump, 880 yards walk, 16lb hammer throw, pole vault, 120 yard hurdles, 56lb weight throw, long jump and 1 mile — completed in a day. This variation was an American product. Scandinavia and Germany had their own alternative versions.

In 1912 the Stockholm Olympics was the stage for the first two-day modern decathlon. It was identical to the present day order, except that on this occasion the discus preceded the 110 metres hurdles. The event was so popular that the competition actually lasted three days to accommodate all the competitors!

The final order of events was eventually settled before the 1920 Olympic Games.

A pentathlon for men was also included in the famous 1912 Games and, despite a change in the scoring system, its format has remained intact — long jump, javelin throw, 200 metres, discus throw and 1500 metres. It has not, however, remained as a major games event.

Scoring Tables

The first set of tables to be internationally accepted were offered by Sweden in 1912, although the I.A.A.F. officially recognised tables for the first time in 1934, produced courtesy of Finland. Adjustments have since been frequent and changes were made in 1952, 1962, and most recently in 1985. It is these tables from which all current scores are taken.

The decathlon has been dominated by only a few nations. Britain has been a very late starter. The U.S.A., with its vast reservoir of talent, produced the first true star, Jim Thorpe, a Crow Indian. He received a cup, donated by the Tzar of Russia, for winning at the 1912 Olympic Games but had to relinquish his medal after accusations of professionalism; he had played minor league baseball. To the credit of themselves and the spirit of multi events his vanquished competitors refused the vacant medal and the legend of Thorpe was assured! He was posthumously reinstated in 1973 by the American Athletic Union, twenty years after his death, and by the International Olympic Committee in October 1982. His family have been given a replica of his medal and he is now officially recognised as equal first!

Scandinavia's then advanced attitude to physical education helped them challenge America's supremacy until 1936 when Glenn Morris exceeded 7000

Jim Thorpe —
lost amateur status and Olympic Medals.

points for the first time (7421). He went on to become a Hollywood ''Tarzan''.

Bob Mathias challenges as the greatest of them all, having won two Olympic golds (London and Helsinki) and retired by the time he was twenty two years of age! He became an American Senator.

America continued to dominate Olympic competition with:- Milt Campbell — Melbourne 1956, Rafer Johnson — Rome 1960, Bill Toomey — Mexico 1968 and Bruce Jenner — Montreal 1976.

Opposition came briefly from Formosa: C.K. Yang, whose amazing pole vaulting broke the then existing tables, threatening Johnson; and from an ever growing European challenge.

Rafer Johnson.

The West Germans first showed their hand in 1964 when Willi Holdorf took gold. They have since produced a string of world class performers including Guido Kratschmer, Jurgen Hingsen and Siegfried Wentz. The first Eastern European winner was Nikolai Avilov of the U.S.S.R. at Munich.

The modern event really took off due to the excellence of Hingsen and Britain's Daley Thompson, for whom the 1976 Montreal Olympics was a learning experience. Since gaining a silver medal in the European Championships in 1978 he has dominated evey major championship for almost a decade:

— Olympic Games	— 1980 and 1984
— World Championships	— 1983
— European Championships	— 1982 and 1986
— Commonwealth Games	— 1978, 1982 and 1986.

Torsten Voss (G.D.R.) was the athlete who broke the golden streak at the World Championships in Rome 1987, followed by Christian Schenk at the Seoul Olympics, 1988.

The World Record, created at the Los Angeles Olympics, still remains in the hands of Thompson with the score of 8847 points.

WOMEN

Women competed in track events in Ancient Greece but little is known. It is shameful that the dark days of prejudice and bias towards women in sport did not start to collapse until this, the twentieth century. In 1922 the I.A.A.F., under pressure, set up a "Women's Committee" but even then Olympic competition was denied them until 1928. Multi events did not become part of the programme until 1964 in Tokyo! The "pentathlon", as it was then, comprised: 80 metre hurdles, shot putt, high jump, long jump and 200 metres, to be contested for over two days. The first gold medal was won by the formidable Irena Press (U.S.S.R.) and the silver by Mary Rand (Great Britain).

In 1976 the 200 metres was replaced by the 800 metres. However this still did not produce a truly all round test. Consequently in 1981 the much more satisfactory heptathlon was proposed and female athletes can now "enjoy" a genuine multi event competition.

The first ever multi event record was created by a Soviet athlete, Elena Vasiliera, in 1927: 100 metres — 13.4 secs., high jump — 1.30 metres, long jump — 4.60 metres, discus — 22.65 metres, and 800 metres — 2.47.8 secs.

The Eastern Europeans appear to have held a virtual monopoly over both pentathlon and heptathlon. However this is not reflected at Olympic level. Only one country, the U.S.S.R., has won more than one championship.

Olympic Titles:-

Pentathlon

1964	Irena Press	U.S.S.R.	5246 pts.
1968	Ingrid Becker	West Germany	5098 pts.
1972	Mary Peters	Great Britain	4801 pts.
1976	Sigrun Siegl	East Germany	4745 pts.
1980	Nadyezda Tkachenko	U.S.S.R.	5083 pts.

Heptathlon

1984	Glynis Nunn	Australia	6390 pts.
1988	Jackie Joyner	U.S.A.	7291 pts.

World Record:-

Heptathlon — Jackie Joyner-Kersee, 7291 points

Mary Peters (Northern Ireland), 1972 Olympic Pentathlon Champion, pips Ann Wilson (England) at 1970 Commonwealth Games, Edinburgh.

A BRIEF HISTORY OF BRITISH MULTI EVENTS

When the performances of Daley Thompson, Mary Peters, Mary Rand and Judy Simpson are put side by side it would appear Britain has quite a tradition in these events. However, all the athletes mentioned by name in this section, except R.M.N. Tisdall and Mary Peters, were coached by British National Coaches: Geoff Dyson, John LeMasurier, Tom McNab, Ron Pickering, Bruce Longden, Frank Dick and John Anderson. Mary Peters was coached by the late Buster McShane.

As the gospel is spread by devoted National and National Event Coaches such as Jim Talbot and Doug Frampton, and multi events attracts an increasing number of followers, it is more likely that these performances are a firm foundation for a tradition.

The following milestones display the recent development of the event in these islands.

1) 1932 Olympic Games, decathlon, R.M.N. Tisdall (Eire, Shrewsbury & Cambridge), 8th.
2) 1954 Olympic Games, decathlon, Geoff Elliott, 9th.
3) 1959 The first G.B. multi events international versus Belgium & The Netherlands.
4) 1960 C.J. Andrews (Army champion 6643 pts). The first U.K. athlete to train exclusively for multi events.
5) 1964 Olympic Games, Mary Rand, pentathlon silver medal.
6) 1964 The first junior decathlon championships, instigated by Tom McNab. Winner Jim Smith (17) 5953 pts (senior implements).
7) 1965 7000 pts. Clive Long (7143), Guyanan by birth.
8) 1969 7903 pts. Peter Gabbett, European Championships, 6th.

9) 1972 Olympic Games, Mary Peters, pentathlon gold medal.

10) 1975 Five Star decathlon/pentathlon course, Crystal Palace. Inquisitive 16-year-old D. Thompson turns up!

11) 1977 Great Britain v. Spain v. Italy v. Holland (decathlon). First time the complete G.B. team exceeded 7000 pts.

12) 1980 Olympic Games, Daley Thompson, decathlon gold medal.

13) 1984 Olympic Games, Great Britain had three representatives in the decathlon. Daley Thompson, decathlon gold medal.

14) 1988 Olympic Games, Great Britain had three representatives in both the heptathlon and decathlon.

British Records at the end of 1989:-

Heptathlon	6623	Judy Simpson	(1986)
Decathlon	8847	Daley Thompson	(1984)

Brad McStravick, second British Athlete to achieve 8000 pts in the Decathlon — Los Angeles 1984.

Mary Rand and Coach John Le Masurier.

RULES FOR COMBINED EVENTS COMPETITION

The I.A.A.F. Handbook includes the following under rule 195, combined events competitions:-

MEN

The Decathlon consists of ten events which shall be held on two consecutive days in the following order:

First day — 100 metres; long jump; putting the shot; high jump and 400 metres.

Second day — 110 metres hurdles; throwing the discus; pole vault; throwing the javelin; and 1500 metres.

WOMEN

The Heptathlon consists of seven events which shall be held on two consecutive days in the following order:

First day — 100 metres hurdles; high jump; putting the shot; 200 metres.

Second day — long jump; throwing the javelin; 800 metres.

As a result of studying the handbook it can be seen that each individual event has its own rules of competition, but it is important to appreciate that the contents of this rule, 195, overrule the individual event rules on occasions:

Rule 6

(a) In the long jump and each of the throwing events, each of the competitors shall be allowed THREE trials only.

(c) In the running events and the hurdles, a competitor shall be disqualified in any event in which he has made THREE false starts.

Rule 10 deserves some explanation. Failure to attempt to start or make a trial in one of the events refers to athletes who make no attempt to compete. It does not refer to athletes who have the misfortune to fail to record a time, distance or height. Athletes who land the javelin flat three times or, as Jurgen Hingsen did in the 1988 Olympics, have three false starts in the opening event are allowed to continue despite gaining no points in that discipline.

The rule was probably introduced to stop athletes using combined events to gain individual marks in a few specialised events.

Alan Lindop, British Decathlon Team Manager, and British Event Coach (Decathlon) Jim Talbot. Just two of a number of people devoted to British Multi Events.

Face of the Future! Mike Smith (Canada), Commonwealth Games Champion — Decathlon 1990 Auckland.

ALTERNATIVE COMBINED EVENTS

Decathlon and Heptathlon are not the only multi events competitions available. The I.A.A.F. gives recognition to a men's Pentathlon.

Within Great Britain, junior Octathlon competitions are held to encourage male youngsters to participate without the hindrance of the more complicated events, which can hamper initial involvement.

Indoor events sometimes include a men's octathlon and a women's pentathlon.

For those who enjoy particularly severe challenges the ''blitz'' decathlon offers satisfaction. On this occasion all events must be completed within one hour!

Coaches and athletes interested in these alternative combined events should write to their local association for detailed information.

Bibliography

''Factors determining specificity for multi event athletes''. Longden, 1977.

''Decathlon Training for the Novice''. Talbot, 1982.

Decathlon and Pentathlon Booklet. McNab, 1978.

''Specific features of the Decathlon''. A. Krzesinski.

''Training load in the Decathlon''. Kudu.

B.A.A.B. Senior Coaching Course Notes. Talbot and Frampton, 1988.

''Training Notes''. Mike Holmes.

''Training Diary''. Brad McStravick.

Combined Events Annual Report. Max Jones.

Photographs: Howard Payne, Mark Shearman, David Lease.